Economic Alarm Clock
Brink of Your Financial Ruin

I0059864

Edition 2

Pauly Hart
July 18th 2022

This book you have
Maybe it's a book
Maybe it's a saga
Maybe it's an epic
Maybe the best nugget
On money
You've read
Since the book of Proverbs
In the Old Testament
…
Or maybe you're a financial wizard
Going to poke holes in my theories
Good
Do it and teach others
…
However
I'm not saying this book is any good
But it's light years ahead of mediocre advice
It's just that I read a lot of books on money
And I'm just giving you some of the things I've learned
And some things I've learned
In a short pamphlet
…
You may hate the formatting

Or the punctuation
Or the capitalization
Well
Whoops

…

I wrote my first book on money almost a year ago
The Richest Man in Babylon
Continued Stories

…

I wrote it as a labor of love for all mankind
But much has happened in this last year
More than Daniel Lapin could have seen
When he wrote: "Thou Shalt Prosper"

…

It's all coming down
The mark of the beast is coming
Coming soon and very soon
Coming to take us all away
Ha ha hee hee
And land us in the funny farm
Where they seek to make us all
Fat, dumb, and happy
Owning nothing
But proud of it

…

Excuse me, but no thank you

…

Maybe the couple of dollars
You invested in this book
Will help you tip the balance
In your favor
That you may live
And not die
And declare

The Word
Of God

…

The point is
That you've taken this step
This tiny step in your journey
Probably not the first
Hopefully not the last
But if you're going to climb
Mount wealth
Might I be to you a valued sherpa

…

This tiny book
Is somewhat problematic
Because i sought to release it so quickly
From a few blog posts
On the Deso Blockchain
On Discord
On Facebook
And a few other places
But i have to let you know
That the end is nigh
That we are entering into
Another great recession
Perhaps another great depression

…

You might not feel it yet
The Misery Index has been check-blocked
It's not the 1920's
There are no bread lines
Because there's SNAP
Or food stamps
And government phones
But it's only going to get worse

Your neighbors will want what you have
Don't give them any foothold into your wealth
They must earn it even as you have

…

Love your wife, your husband, your family
This is love
Do not foolishly cast your pearls before swine
Foolish altruism is not actual love
Love is caregiving
Love is patient
Love is kind
Love, in verb form, is action towards others

…

This small books will help you love your family
This book is not a get rich quick scheme
This book is an alarm clock
If you read my last book on money
Last year like many others
You know what i am talking about

…

WAKE UP
The day will come where your "money" will be worthless
Because you "invested" it in the wrong things
And not the things that would keep you you alive
You bought liabilities
You ignored assets
You thought your car
Or your house
Or your retirement account
Would protect you

…

Guess what?
I AM NOT YOUR INVESTMENT COUNSELOR
I AM NOT GIVING YOU ADVICE

THESE EXAMPLES ARE FOR DISCUSSION ONLY

…

But if you thought your NASCAR collection
Was worth something
Or your comics
Or baseball cards
Or ceramic clowns
Or whatever other lie
You swallowed whole

…

You thought dollars were safe
You thought dollars were from the government
You thought dollars were backed by gold
You thought dollars would always buy things
You thought wrong
Dollars are fiat
They are fake
They are not wealth
They are a substitute for wealth

…

Wealth is something that stays
when money disappears
Gold has been the best "STORE" of wealth
for the last 5000 years
Land has always been valuable
Because there's a fixed amount of it
And what is done with it changes its value
The land under the Empire State Building
May be more valuable
Than a forest in Madagascar
Because of purpose

…

Value is God's idea
Fake currency is man's idea

Wealth was created by Him
The idea to be able to work to attain wealth
Also God's idea
The invention of paper that can be used to buy or sell
The invention of fractional reserve lending
The invention of duplicitous schemes by a central bank
Man's ideas
Get more creation
Get less invention

…

My wife and I just got out of silver before going into crypto
It's still a great store of value
We made 100% Return on Investment
We brought for $14 and sold for $28

…

All hard assets are always better than fiat
Land, metal, even wood!!!

…

A secondary asset from land is always great
Oil, fish, lumber, metal, water

…

Owning the land
Often gives you the second asset for free
It just takes labor
And some government forms

…

My wife and I have flipped several houses in the past
We've "played the market" with one of them
Doing almost nothing but doubling our money
Two of them we added a lot of value by hard labor
And also doubled our money

…

The best land deals I've ever done
Were in cemetery plots

By reading newspapers

…

I used to own 40 acres of land
In the north Chihuahuan desert
I gave that away
Because I had no mineral rights
No water
No oil
No gas
Couldn't even put up solar or wind
It wasn't even worth the taxes I was paying
Unless coyotes are a valued resource

…

Knowing the value of your resource
Keeps the robber from nicking your pants
Throw away "problem" projects
If they only detract from wealth-building

…

It's a strange notion people don't get:
Capitalism
If I own a resource, it can work for me
I, as a writer, own a lot of IP
Intellectual property
So every story or game idea becomes digital land
It's the application of the implementation
Of those digital assets
Into a usable hard asset
That I can create wealth with
Which generates a passive income

…

Think of my mind as a spring
The water can just flow down the hill as waste

…

Oooooooor

...
I can irrigate my land
And grow rice or hemp
Or tobacco or corn or whatever

...
We just pulled out our 401ks and our Roth IRA's
into cash and are probably buying silver with it

...
The Japanese Yen is at a 20 year high.
Why?
Q.E.
Quantitative Easing
That's horrifying.

...
It's what Biden is doing to the U.S. at this very moment.

...
My wife judges inflation by snack lunch food.
Evidently, Uncrustables' price went from $1 each to $2.
That made it an alarming reality for her.
I don't even know
Her benchmarks are not mine
She's keeping tabs on lunchables too
Two years to halve the spending power
of her dollar actually angered her
I asked her:
"Now do you believe me?"

...
I said: "Let's start buying from restaurant supply companies
For kitchen goods and groceries"
She laughed and said: "good idea"
Biden is more powerful than Trump ever could have been.
Q.E. and helicopter money will starve the under prepared

...
Woe be to yuppies

who do not know how to farm

…

Biden
Joe Biden
The President of the United States
When i say "Biden"
What i actually mean
is the machine behind the puppet
Not the dullard himself

…

I hope you would not believe me that malinformed
That the old man
Who sniffs little girls
Would somehow control
This government

…

I don't even care what you believe about me
This is about my love for your life

…

If I don't warn you
Then I hate you

…

Get ready
The worst poverty the USA has ever known swiftly approaches
Not The US
The USA
Not the corporation that controls the states
But for the states themselves
Namely the people of the states

…

Bad times are here
Worse times are ahead
Woe to women who nurse
Their children in those days

…

I got up this morning and bought some more silver
It was a good price today
I know a couple of markets well
Silver is one of them. some tips that i do is/are

…

Find as close to spot price as possible
Don't purchase any "rare" coins
Don't purchase any unverified mints
Don't purchase junk or rolled coin
Buy .999 (fine)
Buy trusted mint "no-frills" bars
Stay away from "collectors editions"
Get as far away from numismatic as you can
Stick with raw metal
Buy at discount prices

…

If there's a price break at 10 then don't buy 9
Don't buy "the hottest thing"
Buy the most popular thing
Don't buy huge chunks, they are hard to sell.
I prefer buying 1 ounce bars
I buy low and hold hold hold until it's high
When I sell, it's usually at a flea market

…

Or a jeweler
Not a pawn shop
Though i've been wrong before

…

I find a buyer who will buy near spot
I show him one bar and indicate i have maybe some more
I haggle until agreement is found

…

Then

I go and get the agreed amount from "the place"
And then we trade

…

Guess what?
I AM NOT YOUR INVESTMENT COUNSELOR
I AM NOT GIVING YOU ADVICE
THESE EXAMPLES ARE FOR DISCUSSION ONLY

…

Silver is great. it's a non-renewable resource.

…

Metal is God's money
Metal cannot be created by anyone else

…

Gold is not burned up
Silver is burned up as it is used not only in jewelry
It is also used in industry
When silver is used, it is non-replenishable
Silver price point is usually affordable by everyone
"Spot" prices of silver is a market term
It means -
Here's what the value is TODAY
Spot changes by the minute.
Usually each buyer or seller
will add a premium (house charges) to the price.
Sometimes it is 3% or more.
I never sell to a more ignorant person than myself.
I want the buyer to know what they are doing
I will ALWAYS buy from an ignorant seller
I will never buy anything "collectible" or "junk"
Sometimes those "rare coin" deals will get you in the butt
Plus the coins are only 30% or 70% actual silver
Buying "three nine" or 999 or 99.9% silver rounds or bars
is the only thing i do
I'm not in the jewelry business

I'm in a commodities market
This is actual wealth that God created
Silver, gold, platinum, rhodium, palladium are not fiat currencies

…

I AM NOT YOUR INVESTMENT COUNSELOR
I AM NOT GIVING YOU ADVICE
THESE EXAMPLES ARE FOR DISCUSSION ONLY

…

What is numismatic?
Numismatic = collectability... numbered items

…

Here's a really powerful paradigm to wrap your head around
That the WHOLE of the US was involved in this discussion
And no one even hardly knows about it 100 years later???
This is huge to me

…

Free silver -
Free silver was a major economic policy issue
They were in favor of an expansionary monetary policy
Unlimited coinage of silver into money!
Make it tradable on-demand
Do away with the gold standard
Free the silver!
Free the economy!
And guess what?
No one that I know of has ever heard of this movement

…

Silver is great
It's a non-renewable resource

…

Would you like to get some silver?
Becoming a friend with a jeweler is your best option
I had many friend in the business
But things have happened

He got married and sold his business
Then I moved
I haven't found a good local guy in my new area
At this moment, I'm buying on online
The premiums are really bad
Some sites have "new buyer" deals
Every once in a while
I do those

…

I want to get on here and talk about "stablecoins"
That are supposedly stable.
Don't be fooled by the name
They are just as horrible
As the fake (fiat) currency
That they are based upon

…

If it's "TIED TO" a central bank currency
It's part of the beast system

…

The beast system is owned and controlled
By the central banks
The illuminati
Or whoever really is at the top
They control those banks
The central banks control stable coin

…

Free - on chain - block worthy cryptocurrency is
FREE OF THE BEAST SYSTEM

…

Just because it's "digital"
Does not mean it's good or bad
What IS EVIL is marionette joe biden
And his puppet masters
All of their helicopter money

And quantitative easing
Are creating hyper inflation

…

Get out of cash!
Savers are losers!
Cash is trash!!!

…

BUY ASSETS

…

Buy the 5 g's

…

Gold
Groceries
Ground
Gas
Guns

…

These things will save you
When your money devalues
Sitting in the bank
Like rotting fruit
Losing purchasing power by the day

…

Get out of cash
Cash is trash

…

Money is wealth
Dollars are not money

…

I've come to believe that
"IN GOD WE TRUST"
means Baphomet

…

They seek to control us

They seek to own us
They seek to create more for themselves
And give us a false sense of security

...

Getting a higher "paying" this or that is foolish

...

Getting security means jail
Jail has a place called "maximum security"

...

Choose freedom instead

...

Self insured
Self regulated
Self governing
Self employed

...

Are you in control of who God made you to be?
Or are you letting Biden be in control of your "straight path"

...

Security is secure in someone's care.
Our hope is to find that only in God.
Not in any government.
Those who find security in governments
(ore parties like Nazis or Q followers or whatever)
Miss the entire point of living a Psalms 1 and 2 life.

...

When security falls away
Then you have freedom

...

If you want security in man's ideas
Then you lose all your freedom towards God
and vice versa

...

The "security" of first class on The Titanic

Was just as safe as the titanic's hull.
Or the Hindenburg's

…

By finding freedom instead
You leave the doomed system (vessel)
And go somewhere else.

…

The bank closures in China could happen here too
With the new IMF downgrade -
Places like Sri Kanka and Ghana?
These will only be the harbinger of things to come
it will get worse
it will get hard
With the cutback of the breadbasket of Europe
With Russia being a little punk
with the "global pandemic"
It will become harder to decelerate hyperinflation
A Central Bank can't increase
Quantitative Easing
Bailouts
And helicopter money
at the same time that they increase interest

…

 it will kill the country you're supposed to be helping

…

Get out of cash and into a better vehicle

…

I liked Biden for a minute
When my oil well investments skyrocketed stateside.
He's still a crook for putting us on the Paris Accord
But that pipeline cut made me money
Mind you
it was still a DUMB IDEA

…

But you know
When his puppeteers told him
He could get more
Ice cream
And little girls to sniff
He was all for it

…

About the US being in the Paris Accord and it being bad
I will try to illuminate
The position of the US in the world market
Vs. what just happened in the China oil market
The U.S. is an import nation.
We don't export nearly what our GDP demands
It's insane

…

Couple that with our "need"
for Brent and Light Crude
We import from Saudi Arabia.
What did China just do?
They dropped the U.S. dollar
for the Yuan in oil trades

…

THAT'S HUGE!!!
That means all of their oil is now free
Just like ours is now.
Free?
Yes
Because they can print Yuan to pay for it
Just like we can with Fed Bank notes

…

I'm lucky
I know
I'm a money educated person
Living in the "world money" headquarters

in this day and age

…

But you are only
the average
of the 5 people
you hang out with

…

Most of these "Wal Bucks Americans"
Don't even know that the Fed is losing its grip
Wait
Most of these "Star Mart Americans"
Don't even know what the Fed does

…

THE FED is a big printing press
Out of control
We own the world reserve currency
However
HAVE TO start exporting
or even making things again

…

Instead of Hollywood and guns
Right now
It's only Fed notes, Hollywood and guns
Geepers

…

Why do I hate the US
being in the Paris accord?
For a couple of selfish reasons
And several altruistic ones

…

I live in the USA
when the US does stupid things
Against the citizens of the USA
I get angry

The US constantly messes
With the USA all the time
It hurts and it's annoying
It goes back to Nixon and the 1971 Gold Standard
It goes back to FDR in his 1933 New Deal
It goes back to Jekyll Island and the 1913 Beast
The theft of America
The gift to the Evil Hungry Central Banking System

…

Did you think it was a coincidence
That the IRS
Was created the same year
That the New Central Bank was?

…

It's a great experiment
This USA thing
But the more power
the US gives to the Federal Reserve Bank
The quicker it will fail

,,,

A Taiwanese man commits suicide
after losing nearly NT$60 million in Luna coin.
Millenials think that the only asset class is crypto
But it's so new they don't know
What is going to happen with it yet
If you're an idiot
Then diversify
And we're all idiots
Unless God moves our hearts
To encapsulate and protect
What He gave us to keep

…

In all your getting
Get wisdom

...
THE USD is killing
small countries' economies

...
It happened in
Sri Lanka
Turkey
Argentina
Ecuador
It is not done happening

...
The USD is SKYROCKETING in a bad way
Get out of the american petrodollar now
Buy some ACTUAL assets.

...
I just had an [untold quantity] of silver arrive
After "exchanging" it for worthless USD

...
Silver
Gold
Palladium
Rhodium
Platinum
This is GOD'S money

...
It's been my entire life
I was born in 1971
I have never had a day in my life from
A gold backed US Dollar
Since the USD has not been on the gold standard.
Guess what?

...
It's now time to pay the piper
This is the end of the good times

And he is coming not only for your rats
But now will come for your children
Because we did not pay him what he wanted
…
You are seeing the beginning of the bad times
If you are not already secure and sound
I would suggest STARTING immediately
To take measures into your own hands
Out of the hands of governmental control
Governments are controlled
By
THE CENTRAL BANKS
Or
Do you not know the stories of Napoleon and Gaddafi?
…
Sell off your IRA's and 401(k)s
…
Whoops I just lost all my silver
In a tragic boating accident at sea
…
Gold
Guns
Gas
Groceries
Ground
These are wealth
…
Worthless paper with stupid numbers
Dumb "banking accounts" with made up numbers
These are currency
…
Currency HAS TO MOVE to stay "current"
Or like electricity "current"
If it does not move, it devalues

WEALTH can sit still or can move
But it retains its inherent value
It is a STORE of VALUE
Like a battery or a capacitor
Sometimes wealth even grows in value without doing anything
e.g. real estate
Sometimes it gets larger
By doing nothing

…

The way to increase money value
And decrease deflation
Is to have more products
And less paper money

…

But what has Biden and Obama
Yes and Trump
And every president since FDR done?
They have moved work overseas
And printed excess money

…

But guess what?

…

The way to decrease money value
And increase deflation
Is to have less products
And more paper money
Thanks Nixon and Clinton
For propping up China so well so
They could take over

…

If you're into that kind of thing
I talked about devaluing money with my wife
She asked for an example
I pointed out that trump threw money at us

With a "STIMULUS"
I reminded her of the same thing
With Bush jr.
Because in times of economic crisis
People save their money
Both Bush jr and Trump
Threw money at the GEN POP
"Go shopping" they said
What a great maneuver
For all the dumb little sheep
"Free dandelions"
…

Our US Petro Dollar is OVERDRAWN
In 2021 the household wealth
As a percentage of the GDP
OF OUR WHOLE COUNTRY
Is 600%
…

Wait
What
It's not even like it was in 1995
When the FED interest rates came down
And Net worth as a % of GDP
Were around the same
…

OUR FAKE ASSETS ARE INFLATED
IF
IF
They ever stabilize
We will be thrown back to a life
Like it was in the late 1970's
And our dollars are not spending
The way they are now
And that's not EVEN the dollar

That's ASSETS
THAT'S HORRIFYING
In 1981, Fed interest rates were 18%
What?
Insanity
And they're going up there somewhere again
SOON

…

Sovereign debt
Commercial debt
Consumer debt
Are all at all time highs
Now the Fed wants its money back
Crunch
Crunch
Nom Nom
The Fed will eat this country alive
Can you imagine
Jerome Powell
Glasses at the end of his nose
Steepled fingers
With an evil grin?
Just like Jacob Rothschild himself
A fine gift for the Christmas day pudding

…

What will you do when Jerome Powell
Brings rates "back to normal?"
7?
10?
15%?

…

Heavenly Father

…

Help us your children

…
I've been doing some digging
Into the mortgage rates scenario
I've found something interesting

…
The woes of the adjustable rate mortgage
If you have enough people
Who were experiencing positive cash flow
Because of their great rate
That they got at the beginning
But now the loan rate has gone up.
Let's just say it's 10%
not bad eh?
Oh sure it's horrible
Your $1000 debt per month
Just became $1100 per month

…
Eek
That's horrifying
I mean, ok 10% is wacky.
But what if that's over less than a year?

…
Let's say it's just 1% per month
For 10 months
That's 10%.

…
Soon the man
Can't afford that house
Because of negative cash flow
So he has to give it back to the bank

…
Your dollars are not an asset
If the real estate was an asset
You should have refinanced that dude

Into a fixed rate mortgage

...

Listen
A fixed rate mortgage when times are in hyperinflation
Is actually a DECREASED RATE mortgage.
Let that sink in
The more undervalued that dollar is
The easier it is to pay back that loan

...

If the dollar inflation rises 10%
Your loan just dropped 10% of the original percent

...

Roughly.
That's super rough math
But I think you get it.

...

Let's go back to the guy
Who just had to turn in his house to the bank

...

Oh my goodness that sucks for him
But wait, there's more!
Because he isn't alone!
Even 1% of yankee doo-dahs doing this
Create a systemic risk for the banks

...

The banks don't want your real estate!
No!
They're not real estate people!
They want your money!
Not only does the bank not want that land
But they will sell it to the already wise wealthy
For a fraction of what it's worth!

...

But can they?

Can they do it in time?

...

What happens if they do?
Well
The rich get richer
And the middle class get poorer
Or
They are absorbed into a larger bank
Again...
The rich get richer.
But what happens if they can't?
Uh-oh
The market is oversaturated.
Remember 2008?
Yup.
Banks defaulting on their loans from the fed
Now have to close their doors
And ma and pa just lost all that capital.

...

Listen

...

If you have to pay with dollars to afford those loans
Then you are not spending it at starbucks
Or walmart or wherever

...

So products are not being purchased
And the beans in south america that make that coffee
Are not being shipped.

...

So then Jose in Argentina
Can't get his coffee company
To ship to the USA
Jose is up crap creek sans paddle.

...

He took out a Peso loan
Backed against the US Dollar
Well, as i write this
The dollar is up 107.15 on the DXY
That might not mean much to you
But the US dollar index controls most of the world's spending
Because they base their wealth on the u.s. petro dollar
The world reserve currency

...

So

...

If Jose's coffee company
Has a loan for his business
And he is paying
1 to 1 on the Peso loan against the Dollar
Then if the Dollar rises
He is paying now

...

More to pay off his loan

...

And that's not all

...

His bank is also raising his rate
To try to keep up with its loans
So if the USD rises 10%
And his bank matches that to 10%
Effectively
He is paying 20% more for that loan

...

All this and NO ONE IS BUYING HIS PRODUCT

...

So Jose closes the company.
He is broke
Aaaaaand

All of his 100 employees are broke

...

They have no power to do anything
And eventually
Just like what is happening in china
The banks runs dry
And they close their doors

...

And no no one has any money

...

And boom goes the dynamite

...

Oh yeah

...

So let's say that when Jose closes shop
He decides to "play it smart"
And convert all of his (now) worthless Pesos
Into Dollars???

...

It just creates more demand on the u.s.d. in argentina
And less demand for the peso
Making it EVEN MORE DIFFICULT on the dollar
In Argentina
And all over the world

...

AS THE DOLLAR RISES
THE DEBT BURDEN RISES
ALL OVER THE WORLD

...

This is not another real estate crisis
This is a world wide financial crisis
A DOLLAR financial crisis

...

Remember there are five basic asset classes

And yes, you can google them
And I'll be "wrong"
Because google isn't God
And is lying to you

...

Believe me or don't
An asset class is something
That is exchanged for money
It's bought and sold
All over the world all the time

...

Ignore any list
That has "cash" as an asset
Unless you are into Forex currency trading
Then you don't have to ignore it
And are braver than I am
There's some real gains to be had
If you know what you are doing
Back in the early 2000's
My friend and I lost $77,000 in it
Needless to say
I quit doing that

...

Cash isn't an asset
Cash isn't an asset
Cash isn't an asset
Also
Cash isn't an asset
Cash is a liability

...

These are asset classes:
These are the vehicles of wealth
These will move your financial intelligence higher
Putting worthless dollars into other vehicles

Moves your "money" upward and onward
…
Real Estate
Cryptocurrency
Businesses
Commodities
Paper
…
And you can divide them all up into sub categories as well
A lot of people tell me there are more
But I haven't seen them.
…
Real estate has more categories:
Residential
Commercial
Industrial
Agricultural
Raw Land
…
And sure paper can be
Stocks
Bonds
Mutual Funds
ETF's
Investment Trusts
REIT's
Etc...
…
And all that jazz...
…
BUT IT AIN'T CASH
…
And don't yell at me about crypto
Your ignorance is showing

Trust me
I just lost a bunch
In Voyager and Celcius Chapter 11's
Crypto is a hard market
Diversification
And Dollar Cost Averaging
Is the best game there
In my humble opinon

…

And as for businesses?
If you thought that was paper, you'd be wrong.
I mean the actual business
Not a stock option in the business

…

A hot dog vendor obviously has less at stake
Than a CNC hose clamp manufacturer

…

And a hot dog vendor
might never take his company public
Obviously

…

What's that leave us?
Commodities?
Sure
What is a commodity?
Think about it
Anything you can make from real estate is a commodity

…

Silver Gold Coal Diamonds
Or
Wheat Sugar Coffee Corn
Or
Lumber Tulips Christmas Trees
Or

Oil Gas Cotton Tuna

..

That tuna is tricky
Cause that real estate is usually the ocean

...

Even a market
With resource producing animals
That use your land
Honey Silk Dairy Wool Eggs

...

But you get it

...

This is why you'll hear
Pork Belly Futures
on the Kansas City Exchange
And you wonder
"What in the world is that?"

...

Actually, were I a more diversified planner
I'd have invested in July Wheat

...

But I missed my window

...

You really want to grow as an investor?
INVEST!
Your brain will grow
As you learn about your "gold babies"
And what they are capable of doing.

...

In the coming crisis
You can do all 5 at once

...

Get good real estate
Start after a commodity on it

Create a company from it
Sell shares to your company
Mine crypto in a barn on the land

...

Why not?

...

What's stopping you?

...

Bou can still work your 9-5
But eventually
You will need to quit your job
Because you are making so much money
Doing these "other things"
That you don't even NEED a job any more.

...

Isn't that the point of wealth?
To become free?

...

Honestly think about it
If you take your spare time
And sit down and create wealth with it
If you take your spare wealth
And sit down and create wealth with it
Investing it not saving it
Then you win

...

Honestly think about it
If you take your idea
And sit down and create wealth with it
If you take your invention
And sit down and create wealth with it
Investing it
Not saving it
Then you win

...
We have a debt based monetary system
The USA doesn't print money
The federal reserve bank prints money
The federal reserve bank (the fed)
Is NOT federal
Does NOT have reserves
Is a PRIVATE bank
The charter for the fed
Has never been released publicly
No one has ever seen who owns it
Except the owners themselves

...
They print money
Let's just say they print a 100 dollar bill
Guess WHAT
They demand $105 dollars back as payment
HUH?
You heard me
The payment of the $100 is $105 or $110 or more.
It's always more
Why
Why
Why

...
Because it's a rigged system
THE DEBT CAN NEVER BE REPAID

...
The national debt is around 30 TRILLION
The deficit is around 3 TRILLION
We will never ever
Never ever ever
Pay it back
Because it's numerically

And mathematically
And physically impossible

...

If you've only given me 110 bucks
How can I ever pay you back 110 bucks?
Oh
That's easy
Just print more

...

Now you've printed $200 and the u.s. owes the fed $220

...

You remember the french revolution
And their war-cry:
"Feed the poor
Eat the rich"

...

You know why it never worked?
Because the rich made jobs for the poor.
Don't eat your employers
The rich own the houses the poor rent from

...

Call me crazy
But I blame Alan Greenspan
For the Housing Bubble
Because of his artificially low Fed rates
And then he raised rates
And we had the crash
But you can blame everything
That the movie
The Big Short
Talked about anyway
And ignore the puppet-master
Because TRUST ME
If Hollywood tells you:

"Here is the truth"
Then
IT'S SOMETHING ELSE
But
Maybe you wouldn't have ever heard of
Michael Burry without that movie

…

So

…

The same Michael Burry
Has recently been talking about
THE BULLWHIP EFFECT
It's scary
Super scary

…

The inventory to sales ratio
Is over leveraged
That means
That despite certain "shortages"
Stores are holding more inventory
Than they are selling.
Despite
Rising prices on almost all goods
The stores still hold way too much
Than they are selling
Or willing to sell

…

So how does that work?
It's all based on false consumer information
Or false expected consumer purchasing

…

Mister Store owns a store
Mister Cans owns a mandarin orange packaging company
Mister Orange owns a mandarin orange grove

...

Mister UNCLE SAM sends mister consumer a stimulus check
Mister consumer has extra money
He goes to Mister Store
He buys 25% more mandarin oranges
than what he did last month
Mister Store calls Mister Cans
"Hey we've run out of your oranges!"
"Increase the order by 35%!"
Mister Cans calls Mister Orange and says:
"Hey we've got orders!"
"Increase shipping by 55%!"

...

Uh oh
They don't want to run out
However
Mister Store just saw the EFFECT
He didn't look at the CAUSE
Of all the new buying
But he doesn't want to miss out
And have to little to sell
So he thinks he's actually had gains
On a permanent basis
But wait

...

It was just uncle sam
Sending the consumers free money
It's not real growth.
Mister Store is only hurting
Mister Cans and Mister Orange
In the long run

...

The BULLWHIP effect.
A little change

Has HUGE consequences
From over ordering
Based on expectation
Versus reality

...

Now
Put in 5 more links in the chain
And the end guy
Is almost doubling

...

It's the "sugar rush" effect.

...

A temporary effect
From a temporary cause

...

Prices are slashed at the front end
The middle end liquidates and fires new staff

...

Aggregate demand goes down
And people are hurt

...

In 1930 the purchasing power of our 2022 dollar
Was around $20.

...

The purchasing power with each new dollar
Given away by The Fed
Depletes the power of the dollar

...

So

...

The rate of consumer price inflation
Is going up
Up
Up

Up

...

Inflating and inflating and inflating
The CPI is as big as a hot air balloon
Where once before it was just a party balloon
If we see any disinflation
Where prices seem to slow down
From basic needs
Like food and shelter and energy
Then it is a temporary stall
And will not continue in a true manner

...

However

...

Just because you think the bullwhip effect has died
Doesn't mean that it already has died
Because it's just reached the end
And the REVERSE BULLWHIP EFFECT
Is coming back to whip crack snap attack
Remember
Back when the "pandemic" hit

...

[I put that in quotations
To keep it distanced from
Other more real words]

...

Remember that day
Those weeks
Those months
When all the workers weren't allowed to go to work
But all the shoppers
Still had Amazon

...

Hmmm

So demand increased a little
But supply fell drastically
People are still buying
But less people are making
Oh no

…

Quick
Let's fix this problem!
So now there's a mad rush
To make things
Then there is oversupply
Which causes shortages in raw materials
Causing inflation

…

Now

…

Suddenly the rats are let out of the cage
And they go out to eat
And bowling
And to the movie theater
And the mall
And tithe at church
So their pastor can pay the mortgage
And build a new parking lot

…

Then they use up credit and all their leftover cash
Oooh
Even more inflation
Then they are all out

…

So
The people stop buying
But wait

…

We didn't tell the manufacturers that they stopped
So now there's a huge inventory issue
Not to mention the layoffs from the shipping companies
And now we can't get the ships into the port

...

Ugh

...

The reverse bullwhip effect
Causes demand and inflation inevitably to spike
While inventory on essential goods plummets
And IPhones and other unessentials are in overstock
So what will The Fed do?
Give away more stimulus probably
More Helicopter Money
With their depleted dollar

...

As I write this in July 15th 2022
The CPI report just came out a couple of days ago
It's 9.1%
That's higher than June 2008
That's higher than November 1981

...

Celcius and Voyager have closed down
Both filing bankruptcy
They've taken away $5,000 of my dollars invested
Am I angry?
Not really
I figured it might happen
That's why I invested some USD
In each of those types of company
You name the hot wallet crypto app
I've probably got money in it

...

It is a little aggravating

I mean
You know
They were paying some major gains
But
You know what it really is
Market growth and contraction
Tells the public
Who has sustainability
…
My growth pains
Will eventually subside
And the crypto market
Will correct
…
Since Jesus loves me
And has a plan for my life
I will not fear
…
Even if I end up
Living in a van
Down by the river
…
This book is soon over
Tis the season to grow your wealth
If you think it's hard now
Wait until your neighbors are selling you
Their silver spoons
So they can get some groceries
…
Before you put this book down
I want to tell you a final story:
The day that biden was sworn in
I went to the grocery store
I spent $1000 in groceries

And $100 in shelving

…

I installed a "grocery store" in my office
Along the back wall
I bought all the things
I normally buy
Plus extra bagged rice, legume, and bean
A lot of cans
A lot of goods
And sorted it all
Nice and neat

…

We still buy regular groceries
When i see a "super sale"
Like a 10 for $10
I'll buy extra
And put it in my tiny store
And the rest in the pantry

…

Today my initial purchase of $1000
Is worth around $1,200
I've saved $200
Just by buying ahead

…

And don't give me that "expiration date" thing
A good undented can can last 10 years

…

I'm not a prepper
I'm a preparer

…

Take this information
Grow
Learn
Share

Go forth and prosper

P.s.
Please give this book away when you are done
Or
Leave it on the Bus
Or
Somewhere you feel
It will be read
…
By others
Like you

www.ingramcontent.com/pod-product-compliance
Lightning Source LLC
Chambersburg PA
CBHW071423200326
41520CB00014B/3553